# Tutorials in SAS® Business Intelligence:

# Introduction to Web Report Studio

by Renu Gehring

For my husband and children

# CONTENTS

# INTRODUCTION

Web Report Studio is a web based application that is a part of suite of products from SAS Business Intelligence (BI) Platform. Web based means that you use the URL supplied by your SAS administrator to access it. In other words, all you need on your computer is a web browser to access Web Report Studio. Web Report Studio is a reporting application; you use it to view and create reports. Not only does Web Report Studio have a professional look and feel, but it is also intuitive and easy to learn. This tutorial provides an example driven introduction to Web Report Studio. Using a mock hospital discharge data set, we will create and save simple reports and then modify them. The data for this tutorial can be downloaded at the author's website www.ace-cube.com. For an optimal learning experience, use the sample data to recreate the reports we develop in the tutorial.

# THE MANY FLAVORS OF
# WEB REPORT STUDIO

The biggest advantage of Web Report Studio is that it literally molds itself to your job function. Take the example of a manager, a business analyst, and report developer. Imagine these folks on a technical spectrum; the manager has the least technical background whereas the report developer lives and breathes technology. The business analyst is solidly in the middle of spectrum.

**Web Report Studio for All**

| Manager Report Viewing | → | Business Analyst Simple | → | Report Developer All Complex |
|---|---|---|---|---|

Because the manager only needs it to view and understand reports, she will receive the simplest flavor of Web Report Studio. Uncluttered by items used for report construction, Web Report Studio at its most basic has a clean elegant look. It is so easy to learn that the manger can be comfortable navigating it in a matter of minutes. A business analyst who creates simple reports will experience a more beefed up Web Report Studio. Despite its extra features, Web Report Studio remains easy enough for the analyst to master within a matter of hours. The report developer receives the fully loaded Web Report Studio. At ease with other BI applications and the myriad details of a data warehouse, the report developer can utilize the full power of Web Report Studio to build highly complex dynamic drill down reports.

**More Information**: Web Report Studio's ability to adapt its functionality to the job role of its user is why it is considered a role based application. Several other BI tools are also role based.

# DATA USED IN THIS TUTORIAL

## Hospital Discharge Data Set

| | id | hospid | DateOfBirth | DateOfAdmit | DateOfDischarge | Gender | Drg | AdmitCode | DischgCode |
|---|---|---|---|---|---|---|---|---|---|
| 1 | 1295417 | 1258662 | -12956 | 09/17/2007 | 09/27/2007 | F | 73 | 3 | 2 |
| 2 | 1295420 | 1258662 | -5323 | 11/10/2007 | 11/15/2007 | M | 73 | 1 | 1 |
| 3 | 1295424 | 1258662 | 7031 | 09/19/2007 | 10/15/2007 | M | 73 | 1 | 2 |
| 4 | 1295434 | 1258662 | 2220 | 10/25/2007 | 10/26/2007 | F | 80 | 3 | 1 |
| 5 | 1295039 | 1258662 | -11789 | 10/17/2007 | 10/18/2007 | M | 80 | 3 | 1 |
| 6 | 1295040 | 1258662 | -10052 | 10/24/2007 | 10/25/2007 | M | 80 | 3 | 1 |
| 7 | 1295041 | 1258662 | -13307 | 11/07/2007 | 11/08/2007 | M | 80 | 3 | 1 |
| 8 | 1295051 | 1258662 | -5452 | 10/18/2007 | 10/20/2007 | M | 80 | 3 | 1 |
| 9 | 1295052 | 1258662 | -12275 | 11/21/2007 | 11/24/2007 | F | 80 | 3 | 1 |
| 10 | 1295057 | 1258662 | -6677 | 10/22/2007 | 10/23/2007 | F | 73 | 1 | 1 |
| 11 | 1295058 | 1258662 | -11545 | 11/03/2007 | 11/06/2007 | F | 73 | 1 | 2 |
| 12 | 1295060 | 1258662 | -15682 | 10/26/2007 | 10/29/2007 | M | 73 | 1 | 1 |
| 13 | 1295125 | 1258662 | -3558 | 09/28/2007 | 10/02/2007 | M | 73 | 1 | 1 |
| 14 | 1295129 | 1258662 | -12284 | 10/03/2007 | 10/07/2007 | M | 73 | 1 | 1 |
| 15 | 1295131 | 1258662 | -14499 | 10/03/2007 | 10/07/2007 | M | 73 | 1 | 1 |
| 16 | 1295139 | 1258662 | -18225 | 11/05/2007 | 11/06/2007 | F | 73 | 3 | 1 |
| 17 | 1295142 | 1258662 | -15240 | 11/15/2007 | 11/22/2007 | M | 73 | 1 | 2 |
| 18 | 1295143 | 1258662 | -11152 | 11/16/2007 | 11/19/2007 | F | 73 | 3 | 2 |
| 19 | 1295145 | 1258662 | -16478 | 11/18/2007 | 11/20/2007 | F | 73 | 1 | 1 |
| 20 | 1295155 | 1258662 | -15493 | 10/07/2007 | 10/09/2007 | F | 73 | 1 | 1 |
| 21 | 1295156 | 1258662 | -15856 | 10/11/2007 | 10/14/2007 | F | 73 | 1 | 1 |
| 22 | 1295157 | 1258662 | -11745 | 10/14/2007 | 10/17/2007 | F | 73 | 1 | 1 |
| 23 | 1295164 | 1258662 | -2998 | 10/08/2007 | 10/08/2007 | F | 73 | 3 | 1 |
| 24 | 1295171 | 1258662 | -15258 | 09/26/2007 | 09/27/2007 | F | 73 | 1 | 1 |
| 25 | 1295176 | 1258662 | -8026 | 11/06/2007 | 11/15/2007 | F | 73 | 1 | 1 |
| 26 | 1295177 | 1258662 | -17148 | 11/11/2007 | 11/20/2007 | F | 73 | 1 | 2 |
| 27 | 1295186 | 1258662 | -13163 | 09/26/2007 | 09/28/2007 | F | 73 | 3 | 2 |

The **Hospital Discharge** Data Set is going to constitute our data for the purposes of this tutorial. The code that creates the data is available at www.ace-cube.com. Simply copy and paste the code in your SAS window and submit the code to recreate the data set. A few things to note:

Variables in SAS are either character or numeric. The icon to the left of the variable name denotes a numeric variable. The icon indicates a character or text variable. **Id** is the Patient Identifying Record. **Hospid** is the Hospital Identifying Record

If variables in SAS are either character or numeric, then why do we see to left of Dates of Admit and Discharge? Dates in SAS are stored as numeric variables, specifically as the number of days from January 1, 1960. Any date prior to January 1, 1960 is a negative number whereas a date after January 1, 1960 is stored as a positive number. The reason that Dates of Admit and Discharge have the icon to their left and appear as regular calendar dates is that they have a SAS format applied to them. SAS formats do not change the way the variable is stored, only the way it is displayed.

Date of Birth does not have a format applied to it, so it appears to be numeric, confounding our concept of what a date should be like.

**Drg is** Diagnosis Related Group. To those of you unfamiliar with medical data, think of these as disease categories. **AdmitCode** is Source of Admission. This numeric variable relates to how the patient was admitted. 1=Through the ED 3=Physician Referral. **DischgCode** is Mode of Discharge. This numeric variable relates to how the patient was discharged. 1= Regular Discharge 2=Discharge to another facility.

# ACCESSING WEB REPORT STUDIO

Your SAS Administrator will provide you with a URL that is specific to your company. The URL will most likely take the following form: http://*servername.yourcompanyname*.com:8080/SASWebReportStudio/

You will be presented with the SAS Log On Window. You will need to provide a username and a password to log in. Why? Because SAS Report Studio is connected to the SAS Meta Data Server, which needs to ensure that you are an authorized user.

**More Information**: The User name is not case sensitive, but the password is. Once you log in successfully, you will see the following window:

# CREATING A LIST REPORT
# WITH REPORT WIZARD

You have three choices in creating a new report. We will explore the other choices in a later tutorial. Right now, we will choose—New using Report Wizard, which will allow you to build your report in five easy steps.

**More Information**: Prior to use by Web Report Studio, SAS data sets need to be registered in the SAS Meta Data, a task generally reserved for the SAS Administrator.

To select a dataset, use **Select Data Source** and navigate to the right dataset. In above window, the **Discharge** data set has been selected. Notice that you see all variables in the **Available Data Items** pane.

Let us talk about the two icons you see at the base of the **Select data** Screen. *i*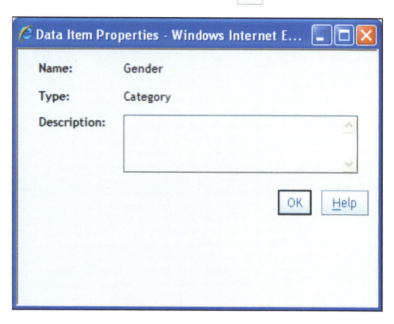

Click on the **Gender** variable and then click *i* icon.

Data Item Properties - Windows Internet E...

| Name: | Gender |
| Type: | Category |
| Description: | |

OK    Help

The pop up window will give you more information about the data item. We know from the pop up window that **Gender** is a category, which is intuitive since we use the values of **Gender** to categorize or separate our analyses.

The icon allows you to find variables. This is useful if your source data contains a large number of variables.

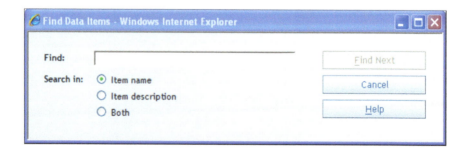

Find Data Items - Windows Internet Explorer

Find:

Search in:  ○ Item name
            ○ Item description
            ○ Both

Find Next
Cancel
Help

**More Information**: If your source data contains a large number of variables, use the **Contents Procedure** to identify the variables you need. This will make it easier to remember which variables to move from the **Available data items** pane to the **Selected data items** pane.

Using the arrows, move all variables over to the **Selected data items** pane. Variables in the **Selected data items** pane can be removed with the delete icon.

Variables can also be placed in different order by using the up/down arrows.

Notice also that the variables such as **id** have the ruler icon to their left.

These are the numeric or measure variables. Variables such as **Gender** have the box icon to their left.

These variables are character or category variables. We tend to summarize measure variables and analyze our data by category variables. Notice that the format on the dates of admit and discharge causes SAS to realize that that dates are not meant to be summarized but rather are useful in grouping the data. For example, we are not interested in finding the average date of discharge, but we may be interested in finding out how many patients were discharged on a particular date. Since date of birth does not have a format, Web Report Studio considers it to a measure, instead of a category.

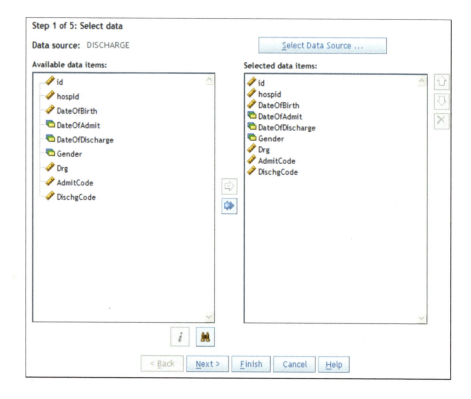

Click **Next** to proceed to Step 2 of the Wizard.

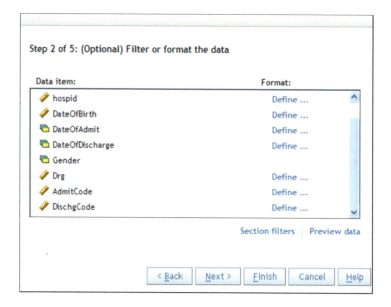

Step 2 of the Wizard allows you to preview data, define formats and specify any data filters. For the purpose of this exercise, we are going to delay these topics till later on in the tutorial. Click **Next** to continue.

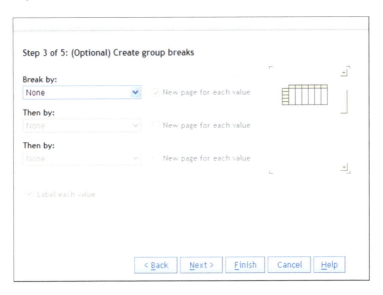

Screen 3 of 5 allows us to create report report by variables. We can check the ⊻ New page for each value checkbox to create a new page for each value. For example, if we choose gender as the break by variable, then our report would be broken out by Males and Females. We could also choose also to begin a new page on each of the two values of **Gender**. For now, skip this screen as well and click **Next** to continue.

In Step 4 of the Wizard, we can specify whether we want a tabular and/or graphical report. We will come back to designing a graphical report later. For now, choose a list report and click **Next**.

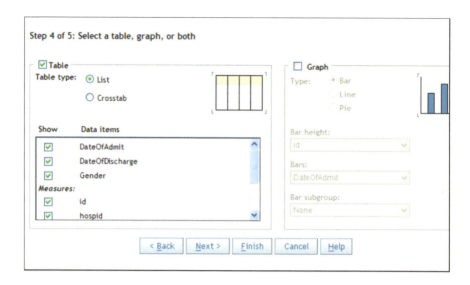

Step 5 allows us to define the header and footer. It allows us to specify an image for a header and footer banner. The SAS administrator is usually responsible for adding images to the Meta Data Server so that they are accessible to Web Report Studio developers. We enter a title for the header and footer and click **Finish** to end.

**More Information**: In order to upload impages for use in Web Report Studio, you need to launch Management Console as an unrestricted user. Go to the Foldert tab and navigate to SAS Folders—System—Applications—SAS Web Report Studio—Common—BannerImages. Right Click on BannerImages and select Add Content from External Files or Directories. After adding your images through Management Console, you will need to restart web container application (JBOSS, WebSphere, or WebLogic) in order for the images to become available.

We see the structure of the report, but not the data itself. That is because, the report is in **Edit** mode. In order to run the report, click on **View** tab.

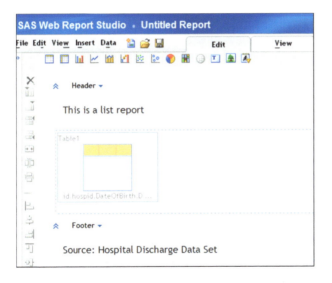

# SAVING THE REPORT

To save the report, navigate to **File—Save As** from the menu. Key in the name of the Report.

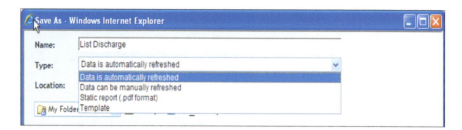

The Report can be saved in several ways. If you choose **Data is automatically refreshed**, then the query underlying the report is run every time the report is accessed. This makes the data in the report dynamic and up to date. However, reports accessing a large quantity of data may take longer to process. If you decide that dynamic updating is not crucial to your report, you can choose **Data can be manually refreshed**. Although the data in the report is a snapshot of the data at the time the report was run and saved, you still have the option of manually running the report to get the most recent data.

The report can also saved as a template, which means that it will be saved without any reference to the data. This is useful if you want to propagate the look and feel of your report. This will be discussed at greater length in a later tutorial about Web Report Studio.

Let us save this report as **Data is automatically refreshed**.

# WORKING WITH REPORT OUTPUT

Report results can be enhanced in several ways to increase the effectiveness of data analysis. Columns can be moved to optimal locations or hidden from view. Data can be aligned to the report developer's satisfaction. Web Report Studio even provides an Excel like sorting hierarchy. Reminiscent of the prowess of the Report Procedure, Web Report Studio allows conditional highlighting of data and calculates column and row based sub-totals and totals. In addition, the analyst can filter report results on the basis of a column's values or rank. As health care cost data tends to be top heavy, i.e a minority of patients make up the majority of the costs, the ability to rank data is useful. Finally, Web Report Studio allows you to export report results to other applications. Let us now examine each of these functionalities in more detail.

# MOVING AND ALIGNING COLUMNS

To move **Id** to the right of **hospid**, click on **Id**, hold and drag to the right of **hospid** until you see a down arrow appear. At this point, you release the click and **Id** is moved to the right of **Hospid**.

This is a list report

Applied filters: None

| id | hospid | DateOfBirth | DateOfAdmit | DateOfDischarge | Gender | Drg | AdmitCode | DischgCode |
|---|---|---|---|---|---|---|---|---|
| 1293612 | 1258662 | 91 | 09/16/2007 | 09/30/2007 | M | 73 | 3 | 2 |
| 1295417 | 1258662 | -12856 | 09/17/2007 | 09/27/2007 | F | 73 | 3 | 2 |
| 1294302 | 1258662 | -14610 | 09/18/2007 | 09/26/2007 | M | 73 | 1 | 1 |
| 1295424 | 1258662 | 7031 | 09/19/2007 | 10/15/2007 | M | 73 | 1 | 2 |
| 1294118 | 1258662 | -19723 | 09/21/2007 | 09/26/2007 | F | 73 | 1 | 2 |
| 1294553 | 1258662 | -16927 | 09/21/2007 | 10/15/2007 | F | 73 | 1 | 2 |
| 1228701 | 1258652 | 578 | 09/22/2007 | 10/01/2007 | F | 73 | 1 | 2 |
| 1294134 | 1258662 | -6896 | 09/23/2007 | 09/26/2007 | F | 73 | 1 | 1 |
| 2586993 | 2517324 | -10380 | 09/23/2007 | 09/27/2007 | F | 153 | 2 | 2 |
| 1292740 | 1258662 | -8036 | 09/23/2007 | 11/04/2007 | M | 80 | 3 | 2 |
| 1294237 | 1258662 | -14216 | 09/24/2007 | 09/26/2007 | F | 73 | 1 | 1 |
| 3815479 | 3775976 | -37741 | 09/24/2007 | 09/27/2007 | F | 240 | 9 | 4 |

To increase the width of a column, simply move the mouse cursor to the line until a cross bow appears, then click and move until you have the desired width. Alignment of the data within a column can be changed by right clicking on the column and choosing the desired alignment.

This is a list report

Applied filters: None

| hospid | id | DateOfBirth | DateOfAdmit | DateOfDischarge | Gender | Drg | AdmitCode | DischgCode |
|---|---|---|---|---|---|---|---|---|
| 1258662 | 1293612 | 91 | 09/16/2007 | 09/30/2007 | M | 73 | 3 | 2 |
| 1258662 | 1295417 | -12856 | 09/17/2007 | 09/27/2007 | F | 73 | 3 | 2 |

Right clicking anywhere in the table gives you a whole host of options. Choose **Assign Data** to change the order of the columns or to hide columns. The latter is especially useful if you want to hide several columns at a time. Remember that these columns are hidden, not deleted. We will discuss

**Assign Data** in more detail later on in the tutorial. Let us go through the other menu items that are available to you by right clicking in the table.

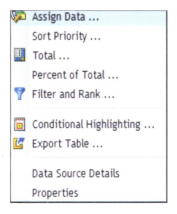

## SORTING DATA

**Sort Priority** gives you the functionality to superimpose an Excel like sorting hierarcy on the data.

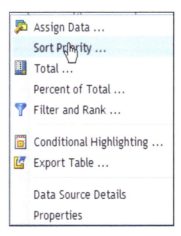

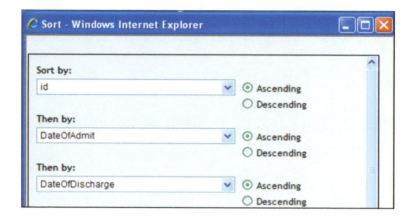

The sorted results are shown below. Notice the 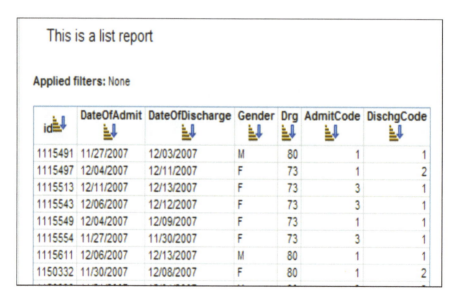 icons, which simply mean that the variables are sorted in an ascending order. Right on any variable to charge sorting to descending.

## This is a list report

Applied filters: None

| id | DateOfAdmit | DateOfDischarge | Gender | Drg | AdmitCode | DischgCode |
|---|---|---|---|---|---|---|
| 1115491 | 11/27/2007 | 12/03/2007 | M | 80 | 1 | 1 |
| 1115497 | 12/04/2007 | 12/11/2007 | F | 73 | 1 | 2 |
| 1115513 | 12/11/2007 | 12/13/2007 | F | 73 | 3 | 1 |
| 1115543 | 12/06/2007 | 12/12/2007 | F | 73 | 3 | 1 |
| 1115549 | 12/04/2007 | 12/09/2007 | F | 73 | 1 | 1 |
| 1115554 | 11/27/2007 | 11/30/2007 | F | 73 | 3 | 1 |
| 1115611 | 12/06/2007 | 12/13/2007 | M | 80 | 1 | 1 |
| 1150332 | 11/30/2007 | 12/08/2007 | F | 80 | 1 | 2 |

## ADDING TOTALS

**Total** from the pop up menu adds row totals.

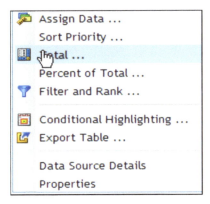

In this report however the row with the totals does not make business sense.

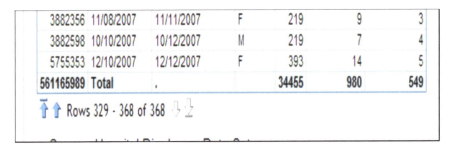

**Percent of Total** is not supported for List Reports, but for cross tabulations. We will return to this later on in this tutorial.

## FILTERING/SUB SETTING RESULTS

**Filter and Rank** gives you an extremely powerful functionality. The results can be filtered through a column's value and rank. For example, in order to create a list report for females only, we would set up a filter for Gender.

More **Information**: After clicking on **Gender** in **Data Items** and selecting **Filter** as the **Type** radio button, you need to click **Browse** to get values. The last action will generate values of **F** and **M**. Use the icon to move **F** in the **Selected values** region.

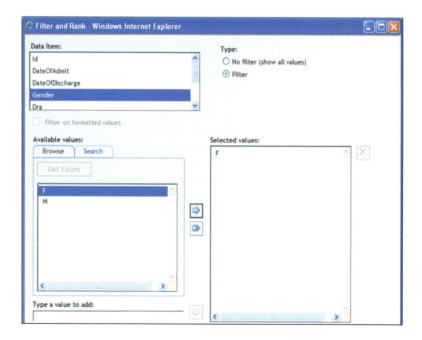

To filter rows of the output depending on the rank of a column, choose **Filter and Rank** and proceed to choose a numeric variable. It would make logical sense to choose a variable that was a metric, such as inpatient or pharmacy cost. Since we lack this information in our hospital discharge data set, we will choose AdmitCode and take the top 10 rows.

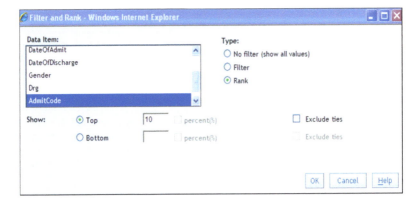

**More Information**: Notice that the percent(%) checkbox is grayed out. This is because we are dealing with a list report, not a cross tabulation.

## CONDITIONAL HIGHLIGHTING

Web Report Studio gives you the ability to highlight data conditionally. For example, assume the values greater than 3 of **AdmitCode** are invalid and we need to highlight this visually with an image. Right click anywhere in the table and select **Conditional Highlighting** from the pop up menu.

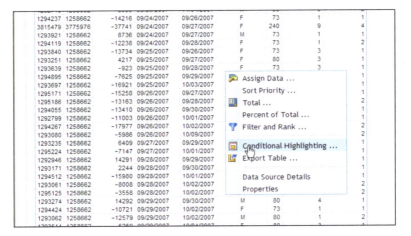

Click **New** to create a Rule that will determine highlighting.

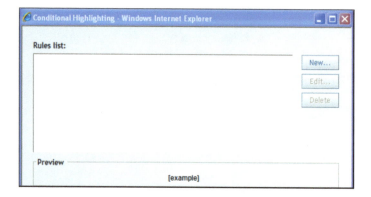

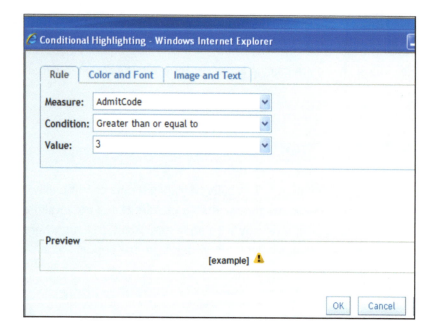

Select AdmitCode as **Measure**, select Greater than or equal to as **Condition**, and 3 as **Value** and then proceed to **Color and Font**.

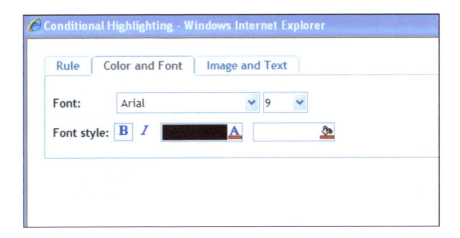

The **Color and Font** tab is used to specify color, font, and text size of the highlighted text. Let us proceed to **Image and Text.**

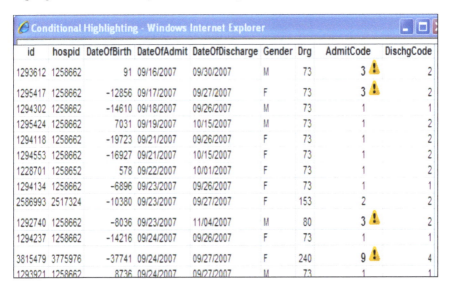

## EXPORTING RESULTS

Web Report Studio allows you to export report results. Right click in the table and select Export Data from the pop up menu.

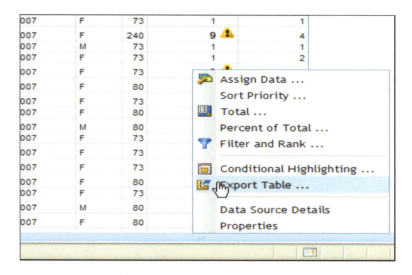

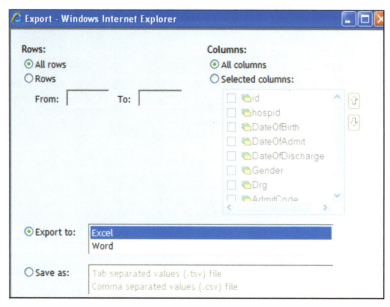

The Export Window comes very handy when you are scrolling through extensive Reports. You can specify which rows and columns to export. Results can be sent to Excel or Word or to a saved text file.

**More Information**: There are two other ways that report results can be exported. One approach is to navigate to **File—Export** using the Menu. The second method is to click 📂, conveniently located with other useful icons in the top bar. Both these approaches lead you to exporting to a zipped file. The drawback to a zipped file is that it has to be unzipped before it can be viewed. The benefit of a zipped file is that it preserves the look and feel of the web report in Excel.

## VIEWING DATA SOURCE DETAILS

Selecting **Data Source Details** from the right click pop menu gives you more information about your data.

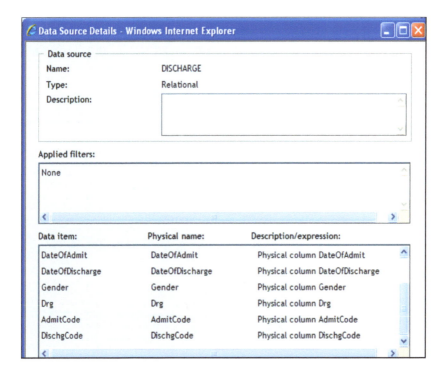

We know that **Discharge** data set is relational. In addition, we know how the data items in the report are mapped to the names of columns in the source data.

## CUSTOMIZING REPORT RESULTS

To customize results, right click on the table and choose **Properties**.

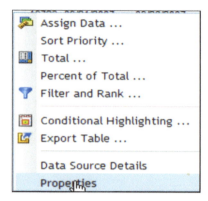

In the **General** tab of **Properties** window, you can enter a title for your table. You can also choose how many columns and rows to display. In addition, you can add row numbers to the report results and choose how many rows or columns you wanted displayed.

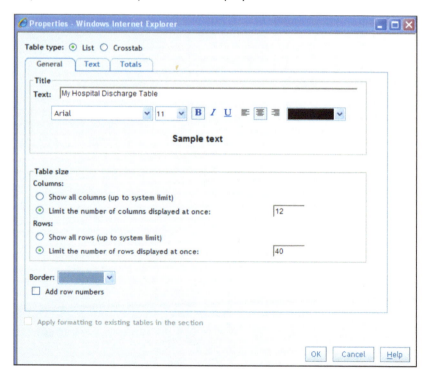

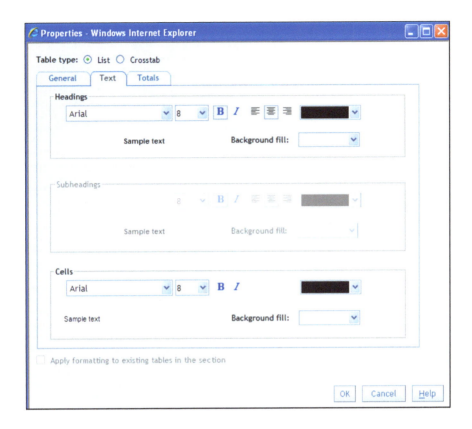

In the **Text** tab of the **Properties** window, you can customize the look and feel of your table headings, sub-headings, and cells.

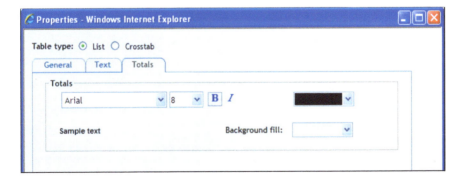

In the **Totals** tab of the **Properties** window, you can specify the look and feel of **Totals** and **Sub-Totals** of the report.

# MODIFYING AN EXISTING REPORT

We have established that the Report Wizard in Web Report Studio allows you to buid a report quickly. In this section, we will learn how to modify an existing report. A number of changes can be made to the List Discharge Report. First the columns can named to impart sense to business users. Second, columns can be given meaninful formats. Third, layout changes can be made to the existing list report. Finally, we can add a brand new section to the report that contains both tabular and graphical reports.

Before we tackle these modifications, let us become familiar with the menu in Web Report Studio. The menu in Web Report Studio is differentiated by whether you are in **Edit** or the **View** tab. This makes sense because there are different things that you can do from each tab. For example, the **Edit** tab allows you to insert a new table or graph. The **View** tab allows you to refresh the report.

**Web Report Studio Menu from the Edit Tab**

Notice that when you are in the **Edit** tab, you see a row of icons.

**Web Report Studio Menu from the View tab**

Notice the absense of the icon row as well as the **Insert** Menu.

Now that we can distinguish between the **Edit** and **View** tabs, let us learn how to carry out common data management tasks.

## RENAMING VARIABLES

In the **View** or **Edit** tab of **List Discharge** Report, navigate to **Data—Select Data**.

The Select Data Screen pops up. Highlight a column whose name you want to change and then click [icon] icon. This icon is located at the bottom right hand corner of the **Selected data Items** pane.

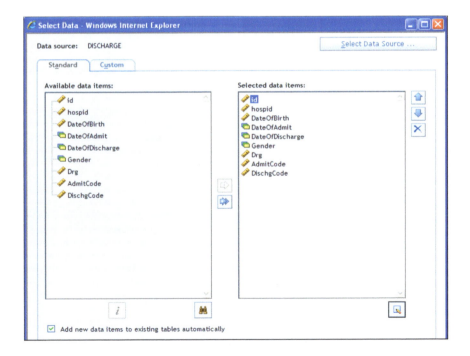

The **Rename Data Item** screen allows you to change the name of the variable.

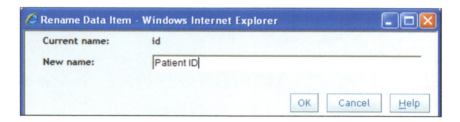

Click **Ok** and you will see that in the **Selected data items** pane, Id has been renamed to PatientID.

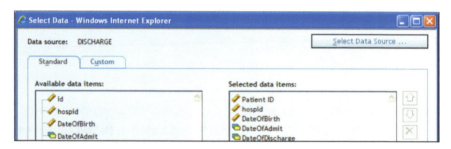

## CREATING NEW VARIABLES

Notice that the above window has two tabs, **Standard** and **Custom**. The **Custom** tab allows you to create new variables.

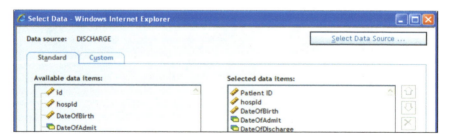

Let us create a variable called Cost, which is defined as twice the values of DRG plus 2,000.

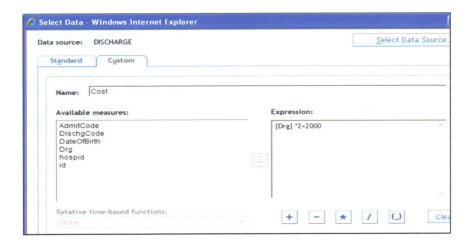

Type in **Cost** in the Name field. As **Cost** is based on **DRG**, bring over **DRG** from **Available Measures** pane to the **Expression:** pane using 🔁 icon. Type in the calculation for **Cost** by using the arithmetic operators available below the **Expression:** pane. Then click **Add** to add **Cost** to the **Custom Items** pane.

**Cost** is now added to the report.

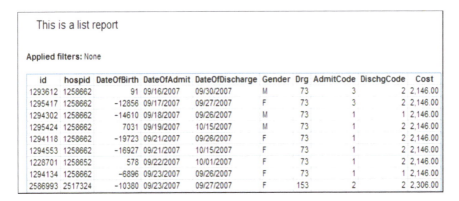

# CHANGING VARIABLE FORMATS

Web Report Studio allows you some functionality in changing the format of a variable. For example, a numeric variable can be given a currency format.

Navigate to **Data—Format**.

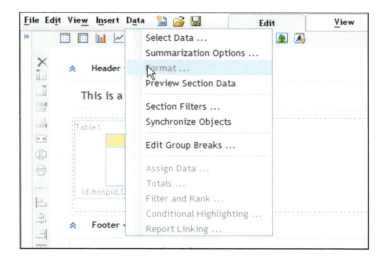

Notice that **Format** is grayed out. This is because a variable has not been selected. You can select a variable in the left hand pane. If the left hand pane is not visible, then click the `»` icon to view the items under the left hand pane. The `»` is located under the **File** Menu.

**More Information:**The left hand pane displays useful information such as **Section Data** and **Table of Contents** windows. **Table of Contents** allows you to navigate to different sections of the report. We will learn about creating report sections shortly.

Columns from **Discharge** data set are listed under **Section Data.** We will Select **Cost** and give it the currency format.

In the **Edit** tab, select **Cost** and Select **Format** from the **Data** Menu.

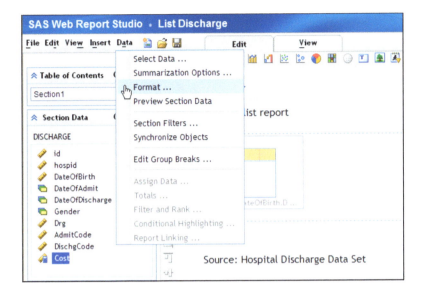

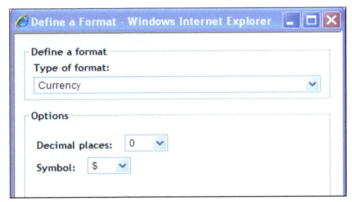

The currency format has been applied to **Cost**.

| id | hospid | DateOfBirth | DateOfAdmit | DateOfDischarge | Gender | Drg | AdmitCode | DischgCode | Cost |
|----|--------|-------------|-------------|-----------------|--------|-----|-----------|------------|------|
| 1293612 | 1258662 | 91 | 09/16/2007 | 09/30/2007 | M | 73 | 3 | 2 | $146,000 |
| 1295417 | 1258662 | -12856 | 09/17/2007 | 09/27/2007 | F | 73 | 3 | 2 | $146,000 |
| 1294302 | 1258662 | -14610 | 09/18/2007 | 09/26/2007 | M | 73 | 1 | 1 | $146,000 |
| 1295424 | 1258662 | 7031 | 09/19/2007 | 10/15/2007 | M | 73 | 1 | 2 | $146,000 |
| 1294118 | 1258662 | -19723 | 09/21/2007 | 09/26/2007 | F | 73 | 1 | 2 | $146,000 |
| 1294553 | 1258662 | -16927 | 09/21/2007 | 10/15/2007 | F | 73 | 1 | 2 | $146,000 |
| 1228701 | 1258652 | 578 | 09/22/2007 | 10/01/2007 | F | 73 | 1 | 2 | $146,000 |
| 1294134 | 1258662 | -6896 | 09/23/2007 | 09/26/2007 | F | 73 | 1 | 1 | $146,000 |
| 2586993 | 2517324 | -10380 | 09/23/2007 | 09/27/2007 | F | 153 | 2 | 2 | $306,000 |
| 1292740 | 1258662 | -8036 | 09/23/2007 | 11/04/2007 | M | 80 | 3 | 2 | $160,000 |
| 1294237 | 1258662 | -14216 | 09/24/2007 | 09/26/2007 | F | 73 | 1 | 1 | $146,000 |
| 3815479 | 3775976 | -37741 | 09/24/2007 | 09/27/2007 | F | 240 | 9 | 4 | $480,000 |
| 1293921 | 1258662 | 8736 | 09/24/2007 | 09/27/2007 | M | 73 | 1 | 1 | $146,000 |
| 1294119 | 1258662 | -12238 | 09/24/2007 | 09/28/2007 | F | 73 | 1 | 2 | $146,000 |

# ADDING A GRAPH TO YOUR TABULAR REPORT

A key strength of Web Report Studio is that it gives you full control over your reporting real estate. This means that you can mix and match graphical as well as tabular reports in your online viewing area.

Currently, we have Table 1 in our entire online real estate. Let us see how we can add a graphical report as well. There are various possibilies, one of which is highlighted below.

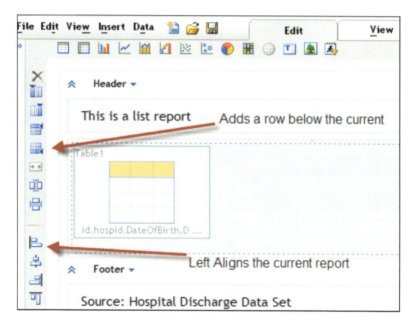

Using the ▦ icon, we add a row to the current layout.
Then click the ● icon to insert a pie chart.

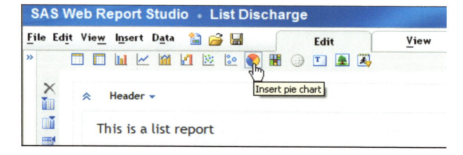

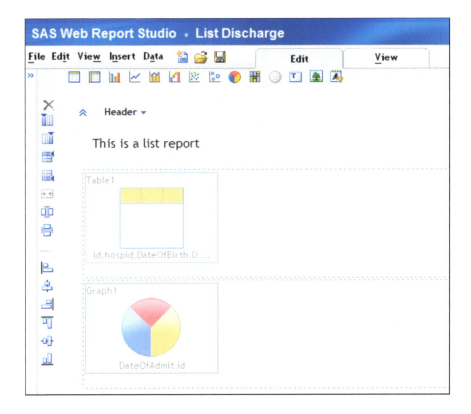

Let us figure out how **Cost** varies with **Gender**. Right click the pie chart and select **Assign Data**.

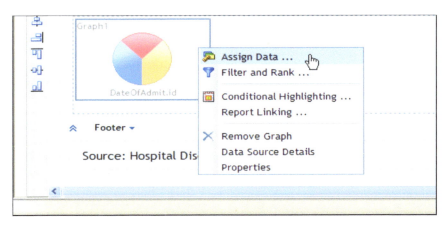

Click on **ID** so that is is highlighted, then move it from **Segment Size** to **Hidden** using **Move Items**. Similarly, move **Date of Admit** to **Hidden**. Alternately, you can also drag and drop to move columns. We need a numeric variable or measure in **Segment Size** and a category in **Segments**. For the purpose of this exercise, let us move **Cost** to **Segment Size** and Gender to **Segments**.

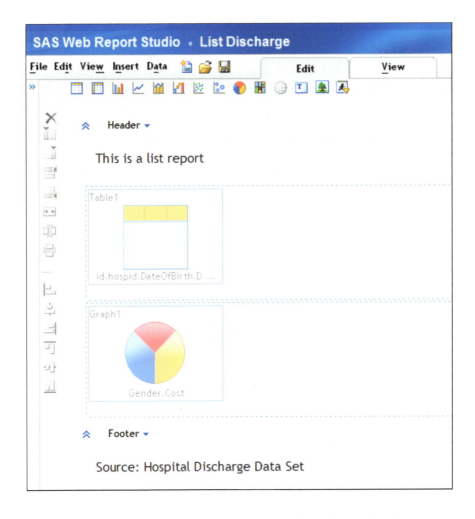

Click on **View** to look at both the tabular as well as the graphical reports.

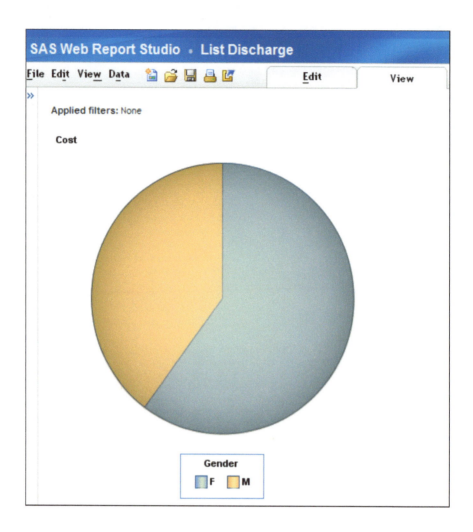

## ADDING SECTIONS TO A REPORT

In addition to dividing up your online real estate into columns and rows, Web Report Studio gives you the ability to insert additional sections, thereby multiplying your total reporting area.

There are several ways to insert a new section. An easy way is to navigate to **Insert—New Section** in the **Edit** tab.

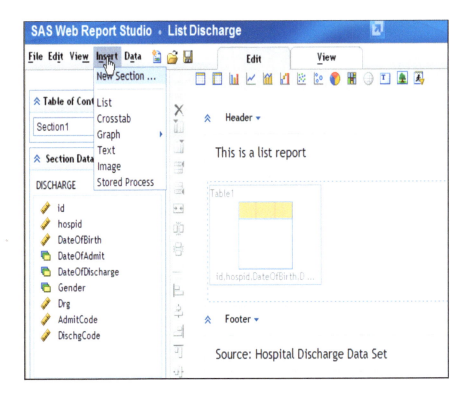

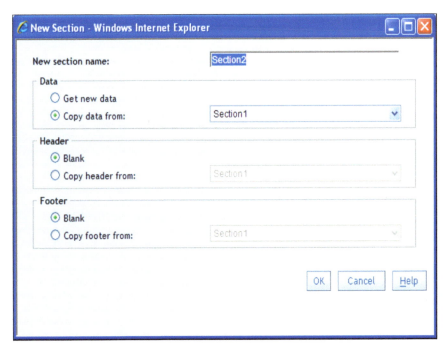

You can choose **Get new data**, if you want the new section to be based on data different from Discharge data. For now, let us choose **Copy Data From Section 1**.

We want to create a new cross tabulation report, so we drag and drop 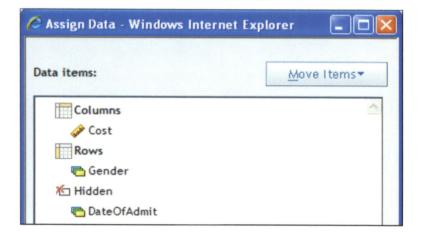 into our report layout. Notice that by default we are given two columns and rows to work with.

Let us create a cross tabulation of **Gender** by **Cost**. Right click to **Assign Data** and move all but Cost from **Columns** to **Hidden**. Move all columns except **Gender** to **Hidden**.

Recall that Web Report Studio allows you to compute **Percent of Total** for cross tabulations. Right click the table and choose **Percent of Total**.

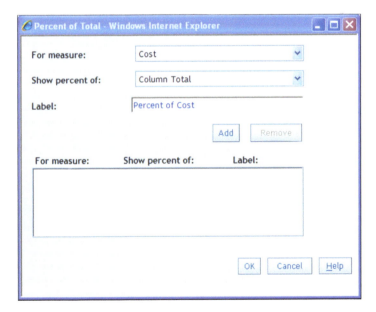

Click **Add** and click **OK**.

You can also use **Filter and Rank** to more sophisticated analysis. Assume that we want to examine the cost of the top 10% discharges for males and females. Right click to **Filter and Rank** and choose the **Measure Filter or Rank** tab.

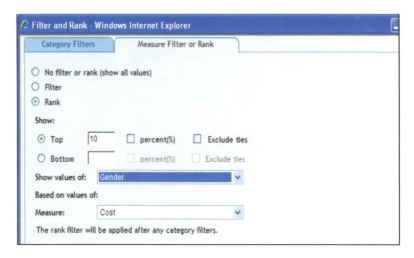

You can toggle between sections using using the **Table of Contents** pane. To carry out household management tasks such as renaming or reordering sections, go the the **Edit** Tab and choose **Options** from **Table of Contents** pane.

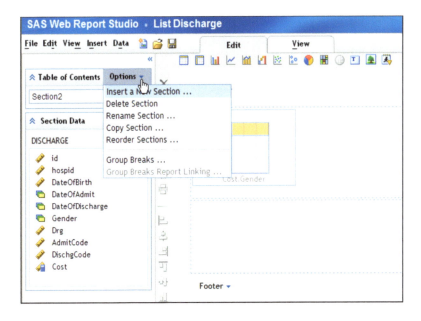

## CHANGING REPORT STYLE

Web Report Studio gives you the ability to change your report look and feel. This can be done in two ways. The first is to navigate to **View—Report Style**. Choose the style you prefer.

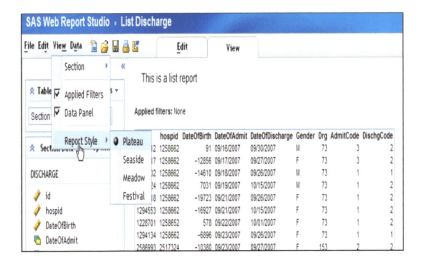

The second method is to navigate to **File—Properties**. Then click on the **Format** tab.

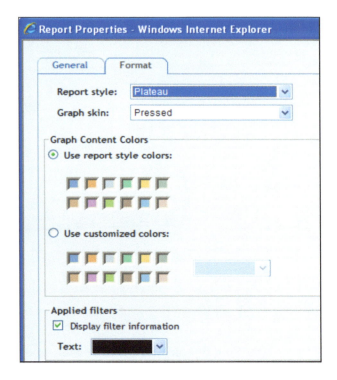

> **More Information**: You can turn off the filter information by unchecking the **Display filter information** checkbox.

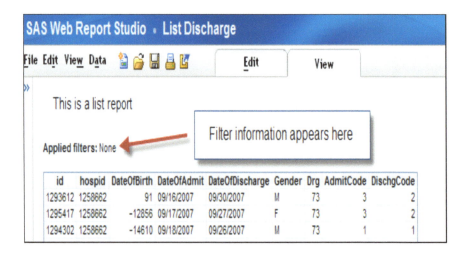

# CONCLUSION

This tutorial has provided an example driven introduction to Web Report Studio. Using the Report Wizard, we created a list report. We worked with the report results using the easy menu functionality in Web Report Studio. Next, we added a graph to the list report. Finally, we added another section containing a cross tabular report.

# TUTORIALS IN SAS BUSINESS INTELLIENCE SERIES

▶ Introduction to Web Report Studio
▶ Creating and Using SAS Stored Processes
▶ Information Maps with SAS Information Map Studio
▶ Advanced Web Reports with Web Report Studio
▶ OLAP Cubes with SAS OLAP Cube Studio
▶ Introduction to Executive Dashboards with SAS Dashboard and Information Delivery Portal

# TUTORIALS IN SAS PROGRAMMING SERIES

▶ Introductory Topics in SAS Programming
▶ Intermediate Topics in SAS Programming
▶ Reporting in SAS: The Tabulate and Report Procedures
▶ Introduction to Macro Programming
▶ Advanced Macro Programming
▶ The Power of Proc SQL
▶ Advanced Data Step Programming
▶ Advanced Data Manipulation

www.ingramcontent.com/pod-product-compliance
Lightning Source LLC
Chambersburg PA
CBHW041146050326
40689CB00001B/506